DE COLORES

A TRADITIONAL SPANISH SONG
PICTURES BY DAVE BLANCHETTE

McGraw Hill Wright Group

www.WrightGroup.com

 **Wright Group**

Send all inquiries to:
Wright Group/McGraw-Hill
P.O. Box 812960
Chicago, IL 60681

ISBN 0-07-572415-4

 6 7 8 9 QST 09 08 07 06 05

*The **McGraw·Hill** Companies*

DE COLORES

De colores,

4

5

bright with colors
the mountains and
valleys dress up in
the springtime.

De colores,

de colores

bright with colors all the little
birds fill the skies in the daytime.
De colores,

bright with colors the
rainbow brings joy
with the glory of
spring.

14

And a bright love with
colors has found us with
peace all around us that
makes our hearts sing.

16

Hear the rooster, hear rooster singing kiri, kiri, kiri, kiri, kiri.

In the morning, in the morning the hen sings her cara, cara, cara, cara, cara.

All day singing, baby chicks all day sing pío, pío, pío, pío, pí.

18

And a bright love with
colors has found us with
peace all around us that
makes our hearts sing.

20

And a bright love with colors has found us with peace all around us that makes our hearts sing.

And a bright love with colors has found us with peace all around us that makes our hearts sing.

24